MEDITATING ON THE MYSTERIES OF SALVATION

Meditating on the MYSTERIES OF SALVATION

A Guide to Praying the Rosary with Joy and Dedication

Fr Frank Drescher

VERITAS

Published 2021 by
Veritas Publications
7–8 Lower Abbey Street
Dublin 1
Ireland
publications@veritas.ie
www.veritas.ie

ISBN: 978 1 84730 987 7

10 9 8 7 6 5 4 3 2 1

Designed and typeset by Padraig McCormack, Veritas
Printed in the Republic of Ireland by Walsh Colour Print, Kerry

Veritas books are printed on paper made from the wood pulp of managed forests. For every tree felled, at least one tree is planted, thereby renewing natural resources.

Dedicated to the faithful of the parish of the
Immaculate Conception and St Killian in
Clondalkin Village, County Dublin, Ireland.

Contents

Introduction and Acknowledgements

The way of praying the Rosary presented in this little book goes back to Wilhelm Kleff (1905–1986), a canon who served for many years as parish priest of the cathedral parish of Cologne. He wrote down his scriptural and other meditations for each bead of the Rosary in the booklet, *So bete ich den Rosenkranz gern* ('The way I love praying the Rosary'), on which this guidebook to praying the Rosary is based.[1]

In Kleff's version of praying the Rosary, an individual verse introduces each Hail Mary within the five decades of a Rosary in the following manner:

1. The angel Gabriel was sent by God to a virgin.
    Hail Mary, full of grace, the Lord is with thee, etc.

2. The angel appeared to her and said, 'Greetings, favoured one!'
    Hail Mary, full of grace, the Lord is with thee, etc.

3. Mary was greatly troubled at his words and wondered what kind of greeting this might be.
    Hail Mary, full of grace, the Lord is with thee, etc.

For those who enjoy praying the Rosary by using insertions after 'thy womb, Jesus' in accordance with traditions from Germany and the United States, short verses have been provided at the top of each page that can be used for that particular purpose:

' … and blessed is the fruit of thy womb Jesus, *whom you,*
O Virgin, conceived by the Holy Spirit.
Holy Mary, Mother of God …'

The first three Rosary meditations from this manuscript are largely identical with Kleff's booklet, *So bete ich den Rosenkranz gern*, as mentioned above. In order to imitate Kleff's use of language, the verses are taken from different translations of the Bible, with some minor modifications either of the text, or of the verses selected by Kleff for the different mysteries. These translations are mainly the New Revised Standard Version, Catholic Edition as available on Biblegateway.com, and the Berean Study Bible from Biblehub.com.

In addition, when Kleff composed his little booklet many years ago, the five Luminous Mysteries as introduced by Pope St John Paul II in 2002 were not commonly known yet. I have therefore added them on my own initiative, along with my own little reflections for them, together with an extra set of mysteries known as the *Consoling Mysteries* of the Rosary. This set of mysteries, which is connected to themes from the Acts of the Apostles as well as from the Book of Revelation, has been approved by the German-speaking bishops and published in the official hymn and prayer book, *Gotteslob*.[2]

Inspired by Kleff's Rosary meditations, I have also developed four completely new Rosary prayers. The first I call the *Miraculous Mysteries*, meditating on the miracles of Christ through which he has demonstrated that he is truly *Immanuel*, 'God with us'. The second I call the *Merciful Mysteries*, meditating on Christ's loving mercy for us humans in our weakness and sinfulness.[3] The other two 'Rosary-style devotions' in the second part of this book are based on the Litanies of Loreto and of the Holy Spirit.[4] These four sets of prayers can be used in private devotions, for example, for special intentions such as praying for someone who is severely sick or otherwise in need of support in prayer, or on selected solemnities of Our Lord, Our Lady and the Holy Spirit.

Over the last twenty-five years I have grown fond of Kleff's way of praying the Rosary, because it is rich in variety and offers, in a special way, what the famous theologian Romano Guardini called a 'participation in the life of Mary, whose focus was Christ'. I wish to share this spiritual treasure from my home country of Germany with my many friends from Ireland, Great Britain, the United States of America and from all over the world.

At this point, I would like to express my deep and heartfelt gratitude to Rev. Dr Jeremy Corley, Rev. Dr Enda Cunningham and Mgr Dr Ciarán O'Carroll for their very helpful theological, spiritual and practical advice in the production of this manuscript. My sincere thanks go also to my English-speaking friends Dr Angela Costley (UK) and Mr Dan Button (USA) for their many suggestions and corrections, but also for their inexhaustible patience with me in the process of writing this book.

I wish for this little guidebook to be spiritually fruitful for its readers. May it assist them to pray the Holy Rosary with joy and dedication.

Fr Frank Drescher
Dublin, 2021, in Honour of the Queen of the May.

ENDNOTES

1   Kleff, W., *So bete ich den Rosenkranz gern*, Johannes-Verlag Leutesdorf: Germany, 17th Edition, 2001. (All rights reserved. Used by kind permission of the Paulinus Verlag Trier, Germany, the current copyright owner of that booklet.)

2   No. 4:8, *Gotteslob, Katholisches Gebet- und Gesangbuch, Ausgabe für das Bistum Münster*, Aschendorff Verlag: Münster, Germany, 2nd edition, 2014, p. 40. This hymnbook has been published by the Bishops of Germany, Austria and South Tyrol in several versions and editions since 1975.

3   The author of the following webpage had a similar intuition regarding a set of 'Mysteries of Mercy', but with some differences in content: http://www.reginacaelipress.com/home/the-5-mysteries-of-mercy

4   I chose this term in distinction to the 'original' Rosary prayers, which by their very form and nature are based on episodes from the New Testament and reflect on the life of Christ as seen through the eyes of Mary.

Without [contemplation] the Rosary is a body without a soul, and its recitation is in danger of becoming a mechanical repetition of formulas and of going counter to the warning of Christ: 'And in praying do not heap up empty phrases as the Gentiles do; for they think that they will be heard for their many words' (Mt 6:7). By its nature the recitation of the Rosary calls for a quiet rhythm and a lingering pace, helping the individual to meditate on the mysteries of the Lord's life as seen through the eyes of her who was closest to the Lord. In this way the unfathomable riches of these mysteries are unfolded.

Pope St Paul VI, *Marialis Cultus*, 47.

The Holy Rosary – Basic Prayers

In the name of the Father
and of the Son
and of the Holy Spirit. Amen.

I believe in God, the Father almighty,
Creator of heaven and earth,
and in Jesus Christ, his only Son, our Lord,
who was conceived by the Holy Spirit,
born of the Virgin Mary,
suffered under Pontius Pilate,
was crucified, died, and was buried;
he descended into hell;
on the third day he rose again from the dead;
he ascended into heaven,
and is seated at the right hand of God the Father almighty;
from there he will come to judge the living and the dead.
I believe in the Holy Spirit,
the holy catholic Church,
the communion of saints,
the forgiveness of sins,
the resurrection of the body
and life everlasting. Amen.

Our Father, who art in heaven,
hallowed be thy name;
thy kingdom come,
thy will be done on earth, as it is in heaven.
Give us this day our daily bread,
and forgive us our trespasses,
as we forgive those who trespass against us,
and lead us not into temptation,
but deliver us from evil. Amen.

Hail Mary, full of grace,
the Lord is with thee.
Blessed art thou among women,
and blessed is the fruit of thy womb, Jesus.
Holy Mary, Mother of God, pray for us sinners,
now and at the hour of death. Amen.

Prayers for Faith, Hope and Love (these can be said on the three beads at the beginning of the Rosary):

- We ask Mary our Mother to pray that Jesus will increase our faith. Hail Mary ...
- We ask Mary our Mother to pray that Jesus will strengthen our hope. Hail Mary ...
- We ask Mary our Mother to pray that Jesus will inflame our love. Hail Mary ...

Glory be to the Father,
and to the Son,
and to the Holy Spirit,
as it was in the beginning,
is now, and ever shall be,
world without end. Amen.

O my Jesus, forgive us our sins, save us from the fires of hell. Lead all souls to heaven, especially those most in need of thy mercy.

Hail, Holy Queen, Mother of Mercy;
hail, our life, our sweetness and our hope.
To thee do we cry, poor banished children of Eve;
to thee do we send up our sighs,
mourning and weeping in this valley of tears.
Turn then, most gracious advocate,
thine eyes of mercy towards us;
and after this, our exile,
show unto us the blessed fruit of thy womb, Jesus.
O clement, O loving, O sweet Virgin Mary!

Pray for us, o holy Mother of God,
that we may be made worthy of the promises of Christ.

O God, whose only begotten Son
by his life, death and resurrection
has purchased for us the rewards of eternal salvation,
grant, we beseech thee,
that meditating on these mysteries
of the most holy Rosary of the Blessed Virgin Mary,
we may imitate what they contain
and obtain what they promise,
through the same Christ our Lord. Amen.

May the Divine assistance remain always with us.
And may the souls of the faithful departed,
through the mercy of God, rest in peace. Amen.

We fly to thy patronage, O holy Mother of God;
despise not our petitions in our necessities,
but deliver us always from all dangers,
O glorious and blessed Virgin. Amen.

Saint Michael the Archangel,
defend us in battle;
be our protection against the wickedness and
snares of the devil.
May God rebuke him, we humbly pray:
and do thou, O Prince of the heavenly host,
by the power of God,
thrust into hell Satan and all the evil spirits
who prowl about the world
seeking the ruin of souls. Amen.

PART 1

Traditional Sets of Mysteries of the Holy Rosary

The Joyful Mysteries

FIRST MYSTERY

The Annunciation

Insertion: … Jesus, whom you, O Virgin, conceived by the Holy Spirit.

Our Father …

1. The angel Gabriel was sent by God to a virgin.
2. The angel appeared to her and said, 'Greetings, favoured one!'
3. Mary was greatly troubled at his words and wondered what kind of greeting this might be.
4. 'Do not be afraid, Mary, for you have found favour with God.'
5. 'Behold, you will conceive and give birth to a son.'
6. 'He will be called the Son of the Most High.'
7. 'How can this be, since I am a virgin?'
8. 'The Holy Spirit will come upon you.'
9. 'Behold the handmaid of the Lord. Be it done unto me according to your word.'
10. And the Word was made flesh, and dwelt among us.

Glory be …

O my Jesus …

SECOND MYSTERY
The Visitation

Insertion: ... Jesus, whom you, O Virgin, took to Elizabeth.

Our Father ...

1. In those days Mary hurried to a town in the hill country of Judah.
2. She entered the home of Zechariah and greeted Elizabeth.
3. The baby leapt in Elizabeth's womb.
4. Elizabeth was filled with the Holy Spirit.
5. 'Why am I so honoured, that the mother of my Lord should come to me?'
6. 'Blessed is she who has believed that the Lord's word to her will be fulfilled.'
7. Mary said, 'My soul glorifies the Lord.'
8. 'My spirit rejoices in God my Saviour.'
9. 'He looks on his servant in her lowliness.'
10. 'Henceforth, all ages will call me blessed.'

Glory be ...

O my Jesus ...

THIRD MYSTERY
The Nativity

Insertion: … Jesus, to whom you, O Virgin, gave birth.

Our Father …

1. A decree went out from Caesar Augustus that all the world should be registered.
2. So Joseph went with Mary up to Bethlehem.
3. The time came for her child to be born.
4. And she gave birth to her firstborn, a son.
5. There were shepherds keeping watch over their flocks.
6. Then an angel of the Lord stood before them.
7. 'Behold, I bring you good news of great joy.'
8. 'This day the Saviour has been born to you.'
9. 'You will find a baby wrapped in bands of cloth and lying in a manger.'
10. 'Glory to God in the highest, and on earth peace to people of good will.'

Glory be …

O my Jesus …

FOURTH MYSTERY

The Presentation in the Temple

Insertion: … Jesus, whom you, O Virgin, offered up in the Temple.

Our Father …

1. His parents brought him to Jerusalem to present him to the Lord.
2. There was a man in Jerusalem named Simeon.
3. He was waiting for the consolation of Israel.
4. Led by the Holy Spirit, he went into the temple courts.
5. Simeon took the child in his arms and praised God.
6. 'Lord, now you are letting your servant depart in peace.'
7. 'For my eyes have seen your salvation.'
8. 'A light for revelation to the Gentiles and for glory to your people Israel.'
9. After this he said to Mary, 'This child is destined for the falling and the rising of many in Israel.'
10. Then he said, 'A sword will pierce your soul.'

Glory be …

O my Jesus …

FIFTH MYSTERY
The Finding in the Temple

Insertion: … Jesus, whom you, O Virgin, found again in the Temple.

Our Father …

1. His parents went to Jerusalem for the festival of the Passover.
2. When the festival was ended, the boy Jesus stayed behind in Jerusalem.
3. They started to look for him among their relatives and friends.
4. Then they returned to Jerusalem to search for him.
5. After three days they found him in the temple courts.
6. 'Child, why have you done this to us?'
7. 'Did you not know that I had to be in my Father's house?'
8. But they did not understand what he was saying to them.
9. Then he went down to Nazareth with them and was subject to them.
10. His mother treasured up all these things and pondered them in her heart.

Glory be …

O my Jesus …

The Luminous Mysteries

FIRST MYSTERY
The Baptism of Christ

Insertion: … Jesus, who was baptised in the Jordan.

Our Father …

1. John the Baptist came, preaching in the wilderness of Judea.
2. 'Repent, for the kingdom of heaven is near.'
3. 'Prepare the way for the Lord, make straight paths for him.'
4. 'I am not worthy to untie the strap of his sandals.'
5. 'I have baptised you with water, but he will baptise you with the Holy Spirit.'
6. 'Behold, the Lamb of God, who takes away the sin of the world.'
7. 'I need to be baptised by you, and yet you come to me?'
8. As soon as Jesus was baptised, the heavens were opened.
9. The Holy Spirit descended on him like a dove.
10. 'This is my beloved son, with whom I am well pleased!'

Glory be …

O my Jesus …

SECOND MYSTERY

The Wedding at Cana

Insertion: ... Jesus, who turned water into wine.

Our Father ...

1. A wedding took place at Cana in Galilee.
2. Jesus and his mother were there with his disciples.
3. 'They have no more wine.'
4. 'Woman, what concern is that to you and to me? My hour has not yet come.'
5. 'Do whatever he tells you.'
6. Six stone water jars had been set there.
7. 'Fill the jars with water.'
8. 'Now draw some out, and take it to the chief steward.'
9. He tasted the water that had become wine.
10. 'You have saved the good wine until now!'

Glory be ...

O my Jesus ...

THIRD MYSTERY

The Proclamation of the Kingdom

Insertion: … Jesus, who proclaimed the kingdom of God.

Our Father …

1. After John the Baptist had been arrested, Jesus went into Galilee and proclaimed the gospel.
2. 'The time is fulfilled and the kingdom of God is near.'
3. 'Repent and believe in the gospel!'
4. He went on from there to teach and preach in the nearby towns.
5. Jesus healed many people of their diseases, afflictions, and evil spirits.
6. John heard in prison about the works of Christ.
7. 'Are you the one who is to come, or should we look for someone else?'
8. 'The blind receive sight, the lame walk, the lepers are cleansed.'
9. 'The deaf hear, the dead are raised, and the good news is preached to the poor.'
10. 'Blessed is the one who does not fall away on account of me.'

Glory be …

O my Jesus …

FOURTH MYSTERY

The Transfiguration

Insertion: ... Jesus, who was transfigured on the mountain.

Our Father ...

1. Jesus took Peter, John, and James, and went up on a mountain to pray.
2. There he was transfigured before them.
3. His face shone like the sun, and his clothes became dazzling white.
4. Elijah and Moses appeared before them, talking with Jesus.
5. They spoke about his departure from this world, which he was about to accomplish in Jerusalem.
6. Then a cloud appeared and enveloped them, and a voice came from the cloud.
7. 'This is my son, whom I love. Listen to him!'
8. When the disciples heard this, they fell face down in terror.
9. Jesus came over and touched them. 'Get up. Do not be afraid.'
10. When they looked up, they saw no one but Jesus.

Glory be ...

O my Jesus ...

FIFTH MYSTERY
The Institution of the Eucharist

Insertion: … Jesus, who gave himself to us as Eucharist.

Our Father …

1. Jesus reclined at the table with his twelve disciples.
2. 'I have eagerly desired to eat this Passover with you.'
3. Jesus took bread, spoke a blessing and broke it.
4. 'Take and eat; this is my body, given for you.'
5. In the same way, after supper he took the cup and gave thanks.
6. He gave it to his disciples, and they all drank from it.
7. 'This is my blood, which is poured out for many for the forgiveness of sins.'
8. 'This cup is the new covenant in my blood.'
9. 'Do this in memory of me.'
10. 'I am the bread of life. Whoever comes to me will never hunger, and whoever believes in me will never thirst.'

Glory be …

O my Jesus …

The Sorrowful Mysteries

FIRST MYSTERY

The Agony in the Garden

Insertion: … Jesus, who sweated blood for us.

Our Father …

1. Jesus went with his disciples to a place called Gethsemane.
2. He took with him Peter, James, and John into the garden.
3. 'My soul is consumed with sorrow to the point of death. Stay here and keep watch with me.'
4. He withdrew about a stone's throw beyond them and began to be sorrowful and deeply distressed.
5. 'My Father, if it is possible, let this cup pass from me.'
6. 'Yet not my will, but yours be done.'
7. His sweat became like drops of blood, falling to the ground.
8. 'Were you not able to keep watch for one hour?'
9. He went away once more and prayed, and an angel strengthened him.
10. 'Rise, let us go! See, my betrayer is approaching!'

Glory be …

O my Jesus …

SECOND MYSTERY
The Scourging at the Pillar

Insertion: … Jesus, who was scourged for us.

Our Father …

1. Judas said, 'Greetings, Rabbi,' and he kissed him.
2. 'Friend, is it with a kiss that you are betraying the Son of Man?'
3. The men seized Jesus and arrested him. All his disciples deserted him and fled.
4. They brought him to Annas.
5. Then Annas sent him bound to Caiaphas.
6. 'I do not know the man!' – And the Lord turned and looked at Peter.
7. 'Yes, I am a king.'
8. Pilate sent him to Herod, who mocked him.
9. 'No, not him! Release Barabbas to us!'
10. Then Pilate took Jesus and had him flogged.

Glory be …

O my Jesus …

THIRD MYSTERY

The Crowning with Thorns

Insertion: … Jesus, who was crowned with thorns for us.

Our Father …

1. The soldiers dressed Jesus in a purple robe.
2. They twisted together a crown of thorns and put it on his head.
3. They put a reed in his right hand.
4. Then they knelt before him and mocked him. 'Hail, King of the Jews!'
5. And they spat on him.
6. They took the reed and struck him on the head with it.
7. 'Here is your king!'
8. 'Away with him! Crucify him!'
9. 'Shall I crucify your king?'
10. 'We have no king but Caesar!'

Glory be …

O my Jesus …

FOURTH MYSTERY
The Carrying of the Cross

Insertion: ... Jesus, who bore the heavy cross for us.

Our Father ...

1. Jesus is condemned to death.
2. Jesus carries his cross.
3. Jesus falls the first time.
4. Jesus meets his mother.
5. Simon of Cyrene helps Jesus to carry the cross.
6. Veronica wipes the face of Jesus.
7. Jesus falls the second time.
8. Jesus meets the women of Jerusalem.
9. Jesus falls the third time.
10. Jesus is stripped of his garments.

Glory be ...

O my Jesus ...

FIFTH MYSTERY
The Crucifixion

Insertion: … Jesus, who was crucified for us.

Our Father …

1. Jesus is nailed to the cross.
2. 'Father, forgive them; for they do not know what they are doing.'
3. 'Truly, I say to you, today you will be with me in paradise.'
4. 'Woman, behold your son. Son, behold your mother.'
5. 'My God, my God, why have you forsaken me?'
6. 'I thirst.'
7. 'It is finished.'
8. 'Father, into your hands I commend my spirit.' – Jesus dies on the cross.
9. Jesus is taken down from the cross and laid in his mother's arms.
10. Jesus is laid in the tomb.

Glory be …

O my Jesus …

The Glorious Mysteries

FIRST MYSTERY

The Resurrection

Insertion: … Jesus, who rose from the dead.

Our Father …

1. Jesus descended into hell.
2. On the third day he rose again from the dead.
3. An angel rolled away the stone from the tomb.
4. The women found the tomb empty.
5. 'Do not be afraid. He has been raised!'
6. Jesus appeared to his disciples. He said, 'Peace be with you.'
7. 'If you forgive anyone's sins, their sins are forgiven.'
8. 'Was it not necessary for the Christ to suffer these things?'
9. 'Blessed are those, Thomas, who have not seen and yet have come to believe.'
10. 'The hour is coming when all who are in their graves will hear the voice of God's Son.'

Glory be …

O my Jesus …

SECOND MYSTERY
The Ascension

Insertion: ... Jesus, who ascended into heaven.

Our Father ...

1. 'Go and make disciples of all the nations.'
2. 'Baptise them in the name of the Father, and of the Son, and of the Holy Spirit.'
3. 'Teach them to observe all the commands I gave you.'
4. 'I am with you always; yes, to the end of time.'
5. 'I am going to the Father.'
6. He lifted up his hands and blessed them.
7. While he was blessing them, he was carried up into heaven.
8. He sits at the right hand of God, the Father Almighty.
9. He lives at all times to intercede for us.
10. He will come again to judge the living and the dead.

Glory be ...

O my Jesus ...

THIRD MYSTERY
The Coming of the Holy Spirit

Insertion: ... Jesus, who sent us the Holy Spirit.

Our Father ...

1. 'I will not leave you orphaned, but I will send you the Holy Spirit to be with you forever.'
2. 'When the Spirit of truth comes, he will guide you into all the truth.'
3. 'He will teach you everything and remind you of all that I have said to you.'
4. When the day of Pentecost had come, they were all together in one place.
5. Among them was Mary, the mother of Jesus.
6. Suddenly from heaven there came a sound like the rush of a violent wind.
7. They saw tongues like flames of fire.
8. A tongue of fire came to rest on each of them.
9. All of them were filled with the Holy Spirit.
10. They began to speak in other languages, as the Spirit gave them ability.

Glory be ...

O my Jesus ...

FOURTH MYSTERY

The Assumption of Our Lady into Heaven

Insertion: ... Jesus, who took you, O Virgin, up into heaven.

Our Father ...

1. 'A sword will pierce your soul.'
2. 'Joseph, take the child and his mother and flee to Egypt.'
3. 'Child, why have you done this to us?'
4. 'Woman, what concern is that to you and to me? My hour has not yet come.'
5. 'Blessed is the mother who gave birth to you and nursed you.'
6. 'Whoever does the will of my Father in heaven is my brother and sister and mother.'
7. Near the cross of Jesus stood his mother.
8. 'Woman, here is your son.'
9. 'I am your chosen one. You will not leave me in the grave or let my body decay.'
10. Jesus took his mother Mary body and soul into heavenly glory at the end of her earthly life.

Glory be ...

O my Jesus ...

FIFTH MYSTERY
The Coronation of Our Lady in Heaven

Insertion: … Jesus, who crowned you, O Virgin, in heaven.

Our Father …

1. A great sign appeared in heaven: a woman clothed with the sun.
2. She had the moon under her feet.
3. She wore a crown of twelve stars.
4. She gave birth to a son.
5. He is to rule all the nations with an iron rod.
6. Mary was his Holy Tabernacle for nine months.
7. From her Jesus received his sacred body and precious blood.
8. Under her loving guidance, Jesus grew in wisdom and stature, and in favour with God and man.
9. Jesus resembled his mother and she resembled him.
10. After Jesus took Mary up into heaven, he crowned her Queen of Heaven and Earth.

Glory be …

O my Jesus …

The Consoling Mysteries

FIRST MYSTERY
The Kingship of Christ

Insertion: … Jesus, who reigns as king.

Our Father …

1. 'The Lord God will give him the throne of his ancestor David.'
2. 'He will reign over the house of Jacob forever.'
3. 'His kingdom will have no end.'
4. 'You are the Son of God! You are the King of Israel!'
5. Jesus of Nazareth, King of the Jews.
6. 'All authority in heaven and on earth has been given to me.'
7. Jesus Christ is Lord, to the glory of God the Father.
8. He is the blessed and only Sovereign.
9. The King of kings and Lord of lords.
10. To him be honour and eternal dominion.

Glory be …

O my Jesus …

SECOND MYSTERY
The Foundation of the Church

Insertion: ... Jesus, who lives and acts in his Church.

Our Father ...

1. 'You will be my witnesses in Jerusalem and to the ends of the earth.'
2. The apostles went out and proclaimed the good news everywhere.
3. The Lord worked with them and confirmed the message.
4. He gave instructions through the Holy Spirit to the apostles.
5. They performed many signs and wonders among the people.
6. The people brought the diseased and those tormented by unclean spirits, and they were all cured.
7. The Lord added to their number daily those who were being saved.
8. Christ appeared to Paul and made him Apostle to the Nations, together with Peter, the Rock of the Church.
9. The Gentiles received the Holy Spirit and they were baptised in the name of Jesus Christ.
10. 'Where two or three are gathered in my name, I am there with them.'

Glory be ...

O my Jesus ...

THIRD MYSTERY
The Second Coming of Christ

Insertion: … Jesus, who will come again in glory.

Our Father …

1. 'They will see the Son of Man coming on the clouds of heaven, with power and great glory.'
2. He will be escorted by all the angels.
3. He sits on his glorious throne.
4. He has a golden crown on his head, and a sharp sickle in his hand.
5. To him is given dominion and glory and kingship.
6. All peoples, nations, and languages will serve him.
7. His dominion is an everlasting dominion that shall not pass away.
8. His kingship is one that shall never be destroyed.
9. The Son of Man will send his angels with a loud trumpet call.
10. They will gather his elect from the four winds, from one end of the heavens to the other.

Glory be …

O my Jesus …

FOURTH MYSTERY
The Last Judgement

Insertion: ... Jesus, who will judge the living and the dead.

Our Father ...

1. We will all be changed, in a moment, at the last trumpet.
2. The trumpet will sound, and the dead will be raised imperishable.
3. This mortal body will put on immortality.
4. Then the saying will be fulfilled: Death has been swallowed up in victory.
5. I saw a great white throne and the one who was seated on it.
6. From his presence earth and sky fled away, and no place was found for them.
7. I saw the dead, great and small, standing before the throne, and books were opened.
8. Then another book was opened, which is the book of life.
9. The dead were judged by what was written in the books, according to what they had done.
10. Finally Death and Hades were thrown into the lake of fire.

Glory be ...

O my Jesus ...

FIFTH MYSTERY
The New Creation

Insertion: … Jesus, who will complete everything.

Our Father …

1. 'See, I am making all things new.'
2. I saw a new heaven and a new earth.
3. I saw the new Jerusalem coming down out of heaven.
4. See, the home of God is among mortals.
5. He will dwell with them; they will be his people.
6. God himself will be with them.
7. He will wipe every tear from their eyes.
8. Death will be no more.
9. Mourning and crying and pain will be no more.
10. The former things have passed away.

Glory be …

O my Jesus …

PART 2

New Sets of Mysteries of the Holy Rosary

The Miraculous Mysteries

FIRST MYSTERY
Christ's Power to Heal Diseases

Insertion: … Jesus, who healed the sick.

Our Father …

1. Jesus went throughout Galilee, curing every disease and every sickness among the people.
2. When Jesus entered Capernaum, a centurion came to him.
3. 'Lord, my servant is lying at home paralysed, in terrible distress.'
4. 'I will come and cure him.'
5. 'Lord, I am not worthy to have you come under my roof.'
6. 'Only speak the word, and my servant will be healed.'
7. When Jesus heard him, he was amazed.
8. 'Truly I tell you, in no one in Israel have I found such faith.'
9. 'Let it be done for you according to your faith.'
10. The servant was healed in that hour.

Glory be …

O my Jesus …

SECOND MYSTERY

Christ's Power over Evil Spirits

Insertion: … Jesus, who cast out demons.

Our Father …

1. When Jesus arrived at the country of the Gerasenes, a man who had demons met him.
2. For a long time he had worn no clothes, and he did not live in a house but in the tombs.
3. The man fell down before Jesus and shouted, 'Son of God, I beg you, do not torment me!'
4. When Jesus asked him, 'What is your name?', he replied, 'My name is Legion; for we are many.'
5. The demons begged him not to order them to go back into the abyss.
6. On the hillside a large herd of swine was feeding.
7. The demons begged Jesus to let them enter these, so he gave them permission.
8. They came out of the man and entered the swine.
9. Then the herd rushed down the steep bank into the lake and was drowned.
10. When people came to see what had happened, they found the man clothed and in his right mind.

Glory be …

O my Jesus …

THIRD MYSTERY
Christ's Power over Death

Insertion: … Jesus, who raised the dead.

Our Father …

1. A certain man was ill, Lazarus of Bethany.
2. His sisters sent a message, 'Lord, the one whom you love is ill.'
3. But Jesus stayed two days longer in the place where he was.
4. Then Jesus said, 'Our friend Lazarus has fallen asleep, but I am going there to awaken him.'
5. 'Lord, if he has fallen asleep, he will recover.'
6. Jesus told them plainly, 'Lazarus is dead.'
7. 'I was not there, so that you may believe. But let us go to him.'
8. When Jesus arrived, Lazarus had already been in the tomb four days.
9. 'Take away the stone.' Then he shouted, 'Lazarus, come out!'
10. The dead man came out, wrapped in grave clothes. 'Unbind him, and let him go.'

Glory be …

O my Jesus …

FOURTH MYSTERY

Christ's Power of Provision

Insertion: ... Jesus, who provided for his people.

Our Father ...

1. Jesus went to a deserted place by himself, but the crowds followed him from the towns.
2. When he saw them, he had compassion for them and cured those who were sick.
3. When it was evening, the disciples wanted to send them away to go and buy food for themselves.
4. 'They need not go away; you give them something to eat.'
5. 'We have nothing here but five loaves and two fish.'
6. 'Bring them here to me.'
7. Taking the five loaves and the two fish, he looked up to heaven, and blessed and broke them.
8. Then he gave them to the disciples, and the disciples gave them to the crowds.
9. All ate and were filled; and they took up what was left over, twelve baskets full.
10. Those who ate were about five thousand men, besides women and children.

Glory be ...

O my Jesus ...

FIFTH MYSTERY
Christ's Power over Nature

Insertion: … Jesus, who exercised power over nature.

Our Father …

1. One day, the disciples set out on the Sea of Galilee to go to the other side.
2. They took Jesus with them in a boat.
3. A furious storm came up on the lake, so that the waves swept over the boat.
4. Jesus was in the stern, asleep on the cushion.
5. 'Teacher, do you not care that we are perishing?'
6. 'You of little faith, why are you so afraid?'
7. Then he got up and rebuked the winds and the waves.
8. The storm ceased, and there was a dead calm.
9. The disciples were filled with great awe.
10. 'Who then is this, that even the wind and the sea obey him?'

Glory be …

O my Jesus …

The Merciful Mysteries

FIRST MYSTERY

The Healing of a Paralytic Oppressed by Sin

Insertion: … Jesus, who restored the paralytic.

Our Father …

1. Some people were carrying a paralysed man, lying on a bed, to Jesus.
2. Jesus said to him, 'Take heart, son; your sins are forgiven.'
3. Some of the scribes said, 'This man is blaspheming.'
4. 'Who can forgive sins but God alone?'
5. But Jesus said to them, 'Why do you harbour evil in your hearts?'
6. 'Which is easier: to say, "Your sins are forgiven" or "Get up and walk?"'
7. 'But so that you may know that the Son of Man has authority on earth to forgive sins …'
8. Jesus said to the paralytic, 'Get up, pick up your bed, and go home.'
9. The man got up and went home.
10. When the crowds saw this, they were filled with awe and glorified God.

Glory be …

O my Jesus …

SECOND MYSTERY

The Forgiveness of the Remorseful Woman

Insertion: ... Jesus, who absolved the sinful woman.

Our Father ...

1. There was a sinful woman who came to Jesus.
2. With her she brought an alabaster flask of ointment.
3. She stood at his feet, weeping, and began to bathe his feet with her tears.
4. Then she dried his feet with her hair.
5. She kissed his feet and anointed them with the ointment.
6. The Pharisees judged her because she was a sinner.
7. But Jesus said to them, 'Her sins, which were many, have been forgiven'.
8. 'Hence she has shown great love.'
9. They said, 'Who is this, who even forgives sins?'
10. Jesus said to the woman, 'Your faith has saved you; go in peace.'

Glory be ...

O my Jesus ...

THIRD MYSTERY
The Pardoning of the Adulteress

Insertion: … Jesus, who saved the adulteress.

Our Father …

1. A crowd of people brought a woman who had been caught committing adultery, making her stand before Jesus.
2. They said to him, 'In the law, Moses commanded us to stone such women.'
3. 'Now what do you say?'
4. He said to them, 'Let anyone among you who is without sin be the first to throw a stone at her.'
5. When they heard it, they went away, one by one.
6. Jesus was left alone with the woman standing before him.
7. He said to her, 'Woman, where are they? Has no one condemned you?'
8. She replied, 'No one, sir.'
9. Jesus said to her, 'Neither do I condemn you.'
10. 'Go your way, and, from now on, do not sin again.'

Glory be …

O my Jesus …

FOURTH MYSTERY
The Promise of Paradise to the Good Thief

Insertion: ... Jesus, who pardoned the penitent thief.

Our Father ...

1. When they came to the place called 'The Skull', they crucified Jesus.
2. His executioners cast lots to divide his clothing.
3. Jesus said, 'Father, forgive them, for they do not know what they are doing.'
4. Together with Jesus they crucified two criminals, one on his right and one on his left.
5. One of the criminals hanging there reviled Jesus.
6. 'Are you not the Messiah? Save yourself and us!'
7. The other, however, rebuked him, 'Have you no fear of God?'
8. 'We indeed have been condemned justly, but this man has done nothing wrong.'
9. 'Jesus, remember me when you come into your kingdom.'
10. Jesus replied, 'Truly I tell you, today you will be with me in Paradise.'

Glory be ...

O my Jesus ...

FIFTH MYSTERY

The Restoration of Simon Peter

Insertion: … Jesus, who forgave Simon Peter.

Our Father …

1. After Jesus' death and resurrection, the disciples went out fishing on the Sea of Galilee.
2. Among them were Simon Peter; Thomas, called the Twin, and some others of Jesus' disciples.
3. Jesus stood on the beach, wanting to show himself to his disciples.
4. The disciple whom Jesus loved said to Peter, 'It is the Lord!'
5. When Peter heard that it was the Lord, he jumped into the sea, rushing to Jesus.
6. Jesus asked him, 'Simon son of John, do you love me more than these?'
7. Two more times the Lord asked him, 'Simon son of John, do you love me?'
8. Peter responded, 'Lord, you know everything; you know that I love you.'
9. Jesus said to him, 'Feed my sheep.'
10. Then he said, 'Follow me.'

Glory be …

O my Jesus …

Rosary Devotion Inspired by the Litany of Loreto

FIRST MYSTERY

The Word was Made Flesh Through a Woman

Insertion: … Jesus, who chose you, O Immaculate Virgin, to be his holy vessel of the Incarnation.

Our Father …

1. Hail, Seat of Wisdom!
2. Hail, Spiritual Vessel!
3. Hail, Vessel of Honour!
4. Hail, Gate of Heaven!
5. Hail, Tower of David!
6. Hail, Tower of Ivory!
7. Hail, House of Gold!
8. Hail, Burning Bush!
9. Hail, Ark of the Covenant!
10. Hail, Holy Tabernacle!

Glory be …

O my Jesus …

SECOND MYSTERY

The Virgin Birth of Jesus Christ

Insertion: ... Jesus, who chose, O Immaculate Virgin, to be born of you.

Our Father ...

1. Hail, Virgin most prudent!
2. Hail, Virgin most venerable!
3. Hail, Virgin most renowned!
4. Hail, Virgin most powerful!
5. Hail, Virgin most merciful!
6. Hail, Virgin most faithful!
7. Hail, Virgin most gentle!
8. Hail, Virgin most chaste!
9. Hail, Virgin, chosen by God!
10. Hail, Virgin Mother of Christ!

Glory be ...

O my Jesus ...

THIRD MYSTERY
The Divine Child was Nursed by an Earthly Mother

Insertion: … Jesus, who made you, O Immaculate Virgin, worthy to be called Mother of God.

Our Father …

1. Hail, Mother of the Radiant Light!
2. Hail, Mother of the Son Divine!
3. Hail, Mother of the Redeemer!
4. Hail, Mother most pure!
5. Hail, Mother most chaste!
6. Hail, Mother inviolate!
7. Hail, Mother undefiled!
8. Hail, Mother most amiable!
9. Hail, Mother most admirable!
10. Hail, Mother of our Lord and Saviour!

Glory be …

O my Jesus …

FOURTH MYSTERY

Christ the Lord Hears the Intercessions of His Mother

Insertion: ... Jesus, who gave us in you, O Immaculate Virgin, a most powerful Intercessor in heaven.

Our Father ...

1. Hail, Mother of Mercy!
2. Hail, Most Gracious Advocate!
3. Hail, Mediatrix of Divine Grace!
4. Hail, Health of the Sick!
5. Hail, Refuge of Sinners!
6. Hail, Comfort of the Afflicted!
7. Hail, Help of Christians!
8. Hail, Cause of Our Joy!
9. Hail, Brightest Star of Heaven!
10. Hail, Mother of Good Counsel!

Glory be ...

O my Jesus ...

FIFTH MYSTERY
The Glory of Mary and all the Saints in Heaven

Insertion: ... Jesus, who gave us in you, O Immaculate Virgin, the most gracious Queen of Heaven.

Our Father ...

1. Hail, Queen of the Angels!
2. Hail, Queen of Patriarchs and Prophets!
3. Hail, Queen of Apostles!
4. Hail, Queen of Martyrs and Confessors!
5. Hail, Queen of Virgins!
6. Hail, Queen of All Saints!
7. Hail, Queen of Peace!
8. Hail, Queen assumed into heaven!
9. Hail, Queen conceived without original sin!
10. Hail, Queen of the Most Holy Rosary!

Glory be ...

O my Jesus ...

Rosary Devotion to the Holy Spirit

FIRST MYSTERY

The Holy Spirit is the Power of God at Work in Us

Insertion: … Jesus, who fills us with the Holy Spirit.

Our Father …

1. Together with Mary, our Mother, we pray for the coming of the Holy Spirit.
2. Come, Creator Spirit!
3. Come, Breath of the Almighty!
4. Come, Power of the Most High!
5. Come, Spirit of Holiness!
6. Come, Spirit of Truth!
7. Come, Spirit of Glory!
8. Come, Spirit of Prophecy!
9. Come, Spirit of Adoption!
10. Come, Giver of Life!

Glory be …

O my Jesus …

SECOND MYSTERY

The Holy Spirit is the Spirit of Faith

Insertion: ... Jesus, who grants us the gifts of the Holy Spirit.

Our Father ...

1. Together with Mary, our Mother, we pray for the gifts of the Holy Spirit.
2. We pray for the gift of wisdom.
3. We pray for the gift of understanding.
4. We pray for the gift of counsel.
5. We pray for the gift of fortitude.
6. We pray for the gift of knowledge.
7. We pray for the gift of piety.
8. We pray for the gift of fear of the Lord.
9. We pray for the gift of service.
10. We pray for the grace to love God with all our heart, all our soul, all our mind, and all our strength.

Glory be ...

O my Jesus ...

THIRD MYSTERY
The Holy Spirit is the Spirit of Love

Insertion: … Jesus, who blesses us with the fruits of the Holy Spirit.

Our Father …

1. Together with Mary, our Mother, we pray for the fruits of the Holy Spirit.
2. We pray for the fruit of love.
3. We pray for the fruit of joy.
4. We pray for the fruit of peace.
5. We pray for the fruit of patience.
6. We pray for the fruit of kindness.
7. We pray for the fruit of generosity.
8. We pray for the fruit of faithfulness.
9. We pray for the fruit of gentleness.
10. We pray for the fruit of self-control.

Glory be …

O my Jesus …

FOURTH MYSTERY

The Holy Spirit is the Spirit of Mercy

Insertion: … Jesus, who calls us to works of mercy in the Holy Spirit.

Our Father …

1. Together with Mary, our Mother, we pray to the Holy Spirit to strengthen us in the various works of mercy.
2. For grace to instruct the ignorant and counsel the doubtful.
3. For grace to admonish sinners and console the afflicted.
4. For grace to forgive offenses and bear patiently those who wrong us.
5. For grace to pray for the living and the dead.
6. For grace to feed the hungry and give drink to the thirsty.
7. For grace to clothe the naked and shelter the homeless.
8. For grace to visit the imprisoned and ransom the captive.
9. For grace to visit the sick and to bury the dead.
10. For grace to love our neighbours as ourselves.

Glory be …

O my Jesus …

FIFTH MYSTERY
The Holy Spirit is the Spirit of Hope

Insertion: ... Jesus, who sustains us by the Holy Spirit.

Our Father ...

1. Together with Mary, our Mother, we pray to the Holy Spirit to come and renew the face of the earth.
2. We ask the Holy Spirit to create in us a new heart and mind.
3. We ask the Holy Spirit to enkindle within us the fire of his love.
4. We ask the Holy Spirit to open to us the treasures of his graces.
5. We ask the Holy Spirit to enlighten us with his heavenly inspirations.
6. We ask the Holy Spirit to inspire in us the practice of good.
7. We ask the Holy Spirit to grant us the merits of all virtues.
8. We ask the Holy Spirit to make us persevere in justice.
9. We ask the Holy Spirit to inspire us with horror of sin.
10. We ask the Holy Spirit to lead us in the way of salvation.

Glory be ...

O my Jesus ...